CONTENTS

Protecting the Garden

Genesis 1–3

In the beginning, God made a world filled with every kind of tree and flower, with silvery fish and feathered birds; with creatures of every size and color and pattern. God created angels to dwell in the heavens and people to live on earth.

God loved his people, Adam and Eve, and gave them a beautiful, perfect garden called Eden to live in. It was filled with animals and trees, fruits and vegetables.

"You may eat the fruit from any of these trees," God told them, "except for the tree of knowledge of good and evil. If you eat its fruit, you will die."

One day a snake slithered up to Adam and Eve. "Did God really forbid you to eat from the tree of knowledge of good and evil?" he hissed. "You won't die if you eat from it. You will become just like God."

And they were tempted. Eve took a bite of the

forbidden fruit, and shared it with Adam, who also ate. But as soon as they had eaten, they knew that they had disobeyed God.

God still loved Adam and Eve very much, but because they had sinned, God could not let them live in the perfect garden any more. So God sent an angel with a flaming sword to guard the entrance of Eden so that Adam and Eve could not return.

Pointing toward God

Genesis 28:10-15

Jacob had been traveling a long time, and he was far from home. One night he slept outside in the desert with only a rock for his pillow.

He had the most wonderful dream. Jacob saw beautiful angels walking up and down on a majestic ladder leading from earth to heaven. At the top of the ladder was God.

"I am the Lord, the God of your father Abraham and the God of Isaac," God said to Jacob. "I will give you the land on which you are now lying, and you will have many descendants. I am with you now and I will protect you wherever you go. I promise that I will bring you back to this land."

Jacob woke up and realized that it was more than a dream — he had been in the presence of God!

He took his stone pillow and marked the special place. Then Jacob made a solemn promise: "If God will protect me and bring me safely home one day, then the Lord will be my God — and this stone will be God's house."

Jacob continued on his way, amazed at what he had seen and filled with wonder at God's love for him.

Delivering a Promise

Exodus 3

After many years of living a quiet, simple life as a shepherd in the desert, Moses was surprised by an unusual sight. A bush was on fire! Flames crackled and snapped around the branches in the heat of the day.

Moses went closer, and he saw that the bush wasn't burning up. In fact, there wasn't fire at all — it was the angel of the Lord! Moses stepped even closer. Then he heard his name coming from the bush.

"Moses! Moses!" the voice called.

Moses was terrified, and he hid his face.

"Come no closer. Take off your sandals. The place where you are standing is holy ground," said the angel, speaking in God's voice.

"I am the God of your fathers, the God of Abraham, Isaac, and Jacob. I have seen the suffering of my people, the Israelites, who live as slaves. Moses, go! You must convince the king to let my people out of Egypt."

"But I am no one!" Moses said. "Why would the king listen to me?"

"Because I will be with you," said the voice.

"Who shall I say sent me? What is your name?" asked Moses.

"I AM who I AM, the God of your fathers. My name will not change. And I will bring my people out of slavery into the land I have promised them."

Moses did not want to go to the king of Egypt, but he listened to God. And God kept his promise. After many plagues were cast upon the Egyptians, the king finally freed Moses and the Israelites.

Revealing God's Power

Judges 6

The Israelites were poor and starving and had been oppressed by enemies for seven years. Many people had turned their backs on God.

Gideon, a young Israelite farmer, was working in the fields one day. He thought he was alone, but suddenly he heard a voice call out: "God is with you, mighty warrior!"

Gideon saw that it was an angel from God. He was afraid and confused.

"If God is really with me, then why have my people been left to our enemies?" he said. "I am from the poorest family in all of Israel. What can I do?"

"I will be with you, and you will strike down all your enemies," said the angel, delivering a message from the Lord.

Gideon couldn't believe it. "Is it really you, Lord, talking to me? Please give me a sign so that I can know for sure," he said. "I will return with a gift, an offering, for you."

Gideon fetched meat and bread. The angel instructed him to put his offering on a rock. Then the angel touched the meat and bread, and fire blazed out and burned them up.

Gideon was now certain that this was an angel of the Lord. But he feared for his life.

"Don't be afraid! You will not die," God's voice said.

So Gideon built an altar to the Lord and vowed to trust him.

And just as God had promised, Gideon led the Israelites in battle, and they defeated their enemies.

Providing Food and Water

1 Kings 19

The Israelites had been challenged to choose between God and Baal. God had proved beyond doubt that he was the Lord, the one true God. Baal's prophets had failed to show that Baal existed at all. Queen Jezebel was furious and planned to take her anger out on Elijah, a prophet of God.

So Elijah fled to the desert, afraid for his life. He sat down under a broom tree and prayed to God.

"I've had enough of this," he said. "I can't go on!" Elijah was so exhausted that he fell asleep under the tree.

God heard Elijah's prayer and answered him. Elijah was soon awakened by an angel, who touched his shoulder.

"Wake up, Elijah, and eat!' said the angel.

Elijah woke and looked around. The angel had brought him some fresh bread and a jar of water. Elijah ate until he was refreshed and then slept again.

The angel woke him up a second time and told him to eat and drink some more. Elijah's strength returned so that he was able to escape from Jezebel and prepare for his long journey to the mountain of God.

Glorifying God

Isaiah 6–7

Isaiah, a prophet, was in the temple in Jerusalem when he had a great vision. He saw God sitting on a throne, a great and mighty king, wearing robes that swept down and filled the temple. Above God, Isaiah saw seraphim, heavenly beings with wings covering their faces, wings covering their feet, and wings that they flew with. They were singing,

> "Holy, holy, holy
> is the Lord God Almighty!
> The whole earth is full of his glory!"

The doorposts of the temple shook as the angels sang, and the temple filled with smoke. Isaiah threw himself to the ground.

"Help me!" he cried. "I am sinful and unworthy, but I have seen the Lord God!"

Then one of the angels flew down to Isaiah with a piece of burning coal in his hand and touched Isaiah's mouth.

"This has touched your lips and taken away your guilt," said the angel. "God has forgiven you."

Then Isaiah heard God's voice. "Whom shall I send as a messenger for the people?"

There was only one reply Isaiah could make. "Here am I," he said. "Send me!"

Then God told Isaiah to tell the people of Israel that they must return to worshiping him. And God promised to send a Savior, who would be called Immanuel, which means "God with us."

Delivering from Death

Daniel 6

Daniel, an important government officer in Babylon, was faithful to God. But not many other people in Babylon believed in God. A group of men were jealous of Daniel, angry that a believer in God could have such an important job working for King Darius.

So they devised a plan to get rid of him. The jealous men convinced the king to create a law that prevented anyone from praying to God. The new law stated that people were only allowed to pray to the king.

Daniel could not obey this law, and he continued to pray to God, just as

he had every day. So it was no surprise when he was bound and taken to be punished. King Darius was saddened to see one of his men treated so badly, but Daniel had broken the law.

Daniel was thrown to a den of hungry lions. The door was slammed shut and the lions began to prowl around him. Suddenly the room filled with white light as an angel appeared. God had sent the angel to close the lions' mouths and protect Daniel, God's faithful servant.

Night came and went. At first light in the morning, the king appeared at the door. "Daniel! Daniel! Has your God saved you?" he was shouting.

"Yes!" Daniel called out. "God sent an angel! The lions did not eat me!"

King Darius commanded his soldiers to release Daniel immediately. Then the king issued a new decree: "Everyone in the land will worship the God of Daniel, for he saved Daniel from the mouths of lions."

Bringing Glad Tidings

Luke 1:26-44

Mary, a young girl from Nazareth, a village in Galilee, was engaged to be married. Her fiancé was Joseph, a carpenter.

One day, as Mary was busy in the house, the angel Gabriel appeared to her.

"The Lord is with you!" said Gabriel. "Do not be afraid. God has chosen you to be the mother of his Son. You will have a child, and you will name him Jesus. He will be great, and his kingdom will last forever."

"How can this be?" asked Mary, shocked. "I'm not even married yet!"

The angel replied, "Nothing is impossible for God! You are already pregnant with God's Son. Even your cousin Elizabeth is going to have a baby in her old age."

"I am God's servant," said Mary. "I will do as God commands."

Then the angel left Mary as mysteriously as he had come.

Mary was excited and immediately went to Elizabeth to share the news. Both women were filled with joy over the wonderful things God had done for them.

Filling the Sky with Praise

Luke 2: 8-20

When Mary was close to having her baby, she and Joseph had to travel to Bethlehem. The small town was so crowded that they had to stay in a stable where the animals slept. There, Mary had her baby boy. She wrapped him in cloths and laid him in a manger to sleep. She named him Jesus, just as she had promised God.

The night was cold and dark. In the hills nearby, shepherds were guarding their sheep, warming their hands over a cozy fire.

Suddenly the sky was filled with dazzling light. An angel appeared! The shepherds were terrified.

"Do not be afraid!" said the angel. "I bring good news of great joy! Today

in Bethlehem a Savior has been born. He is Christ the Lord! There will be a sign so that you can find him. He is a baby, wrapped in cloths and lying in a manger."

The shepherds were astonished. What could this mean?

Then a choir of angels filled the sky, praising God in beautiful voices and saying, "Glory to God in the highest, and on earth peace to all people."

The shepherds had never seen such a wonderful sight. "We must go to Bethlehem!" they said.

They hurried to the town and found Mary and Joseph. And there was the baby, lying in a manger, just as the angel had told them.

Proclaiming Good News

Matthew 27, 28:1-10; Luke 24

Jesus grew up and became a carpenter.
He spent most of his life telling
everyone about how much God loved
them. But there were people who
thought Jesus could not really be God's
Son, people who thought they alone
knew the truth about God.

These people were so angry that
they decided to get rid of Jesus. They
accused him of blasphemy, then they
nailed him on a cross to die. His
mother Mary wept. His friends were
shocked and afraid.

After Jesus died, his body was taken down and put in a tomb. A heavy stone was rolled across the entrance.

A few days later, on a Sunday morning, two women went to visit Jesus' grave. Suddenly there was a mighty earthquake, and an angel of the Lord came down from heaven and appeared to them. His clothes were shining like the sun. He rolled back the heavy stone and sat on it.

"Do not be afraid!" said the angel. "I know you are looking for Jesus, who died on the cross. But he is not here. Come and see — the tomb is empty! Jesus has risen from the dead. He is alive! Hurry and tell the disciples that Jesus will be in Galilee. You will see him there."

The women hurried away to share the news, filled with fear and joy. And, just as the angel had told them, Jesus was alive. They were so happy to meet him in Galilee that they knelt at Jesus' feet and worshiped him.

Bringing God's Instructions

Acts 10: 1-8

Cornelius, a Roman guard, was a kind man who loved God and prayed every day. But he had not heard about Jesus, the man who had died on the cross and risen as a Savior.

One afternoon Cornelius was visited by an angel of God who called to him by name. Cornelius was very afraid.

"What is it, Lord?" he asked.

"God has heard your prayers and knows of your kindness," said the angel. "God wants you to send for a man called Peter. He is staying in the city of Joppa with a man named Simon."

Then the angel left. Cornelius told two of his servants and one of his soldiers about the amazing thing he had just seen and heard. Then he sent them to Joppa to find Peter.

Peter was a follower of Jesus. He had just received a vision from God that the good news about Jesus should be taken to all people everywhere. So when Cornelius's men arrived, Peter understood at once: God wanted him to go to Cornelius and share with him all he knew about Jesus!

So Peter left with the men the next day, taking some of his friends with him. Together they told Cornelius and all of his friends and family about Jesus, the Savior of all people.

Cornelius and all who listened there believed and were baptized.

Rescuing from Bondage

Acts 12: 6-17

Not everyone was happy that the message of Jesus was changing people's lives. King Herod wanted all of Jesus' followers to be put in jail, because Herod didn't believe that Jesus had really been raised from the dead.

So Herod took Peter prisoner and planned to kill him, convinced that this would stop the message about Jesus from spreading. But Peter's friends, family, and all the believers prayed for him. They prayed for a miracle that Peter would be set free.

Herod made sure that Peter was watched closely. He placed guards on both sides of Peter, and more guards at the prison entrance.

That night, as soon as Peter had fallen asleep, an angel of the Lord appeared to him. The prison cell was filled with a bright light.

"Quick! Get up!" said the angel. The chains on Peter's wrists broke loose and fell off. "Get dressed! Put on your shoes and coat, and follow me."

Peter thought it was all a dream, yet he did as the angel said. He walked right out of the prison, past the guards, and through the iron gates to the city. Then, just as suddenly as the angel had appeared, he was gone.

Peter ran to the house of his friends, who were still praying for him. He knocked at the door.

"It's Peter!" Rhoda, the servant girl, cried out to the others.

At first no one believed her, but then they saw for themselves. Their prayers had been answered with a miracle. Peter had been rescued by an angel!

✝ ✝ ✝

Many other stories in the Bible tell of angels appearing to humans. Whether they are delivering messages, saving lives, or singing songs of praise, angels are among us.

Text © 2007 Leena Lane
Illustrations © 2007 Elena Baboni

Published in 2007 by Eerdmans Books for Young Readers,
an imprint of Wm. B. Eerdmans Publishing Co.

Copyright © 2007 Anno Domini Publishing
1 Churchgates, The Wilderness, Berkhamsted, Herts HP4 2UB
Editorial Director, Annette Reynolds
Editor, Nicola Bull
Art Director, Gerald Rogers
Pre-production, Krystyna Kowalska Hewitt
Production, John Laister

Wm. B. Eerdmans Publishing Co.
2140 Oak Industrial Dr NE, Grand Rapids, Michigan 49505
P.O. Box 163, Cambridge CB3 9PU U.K.

www.eerdmans.com/youngreaders

Manufactured in Singapore

14 13 12 11 10 09 08 07   7 6 5 4 3 2 1

Library of Congress Cataloging-in-Publication Data
Lane, Leena.
Angels among us / by Leena Lane ; illustrated by Elena Baboni.
p. cm.
ISBN 978-0-8028-5321-9 (cloth : alk. paper)
1. Angels — Biblical teaching — Juvenile literature. I. Baboni, Elena. II. Title.
BS680.A48L36 2007
220.9'505--dc22
2006029715

Text type set in Fritz Quadrata
Illustrations created with acrylics